What are **Religions** and **Worldviews?**

An introduction to beliefs around the world

Deborah Lock

LION
CHILDREN'S

Text by Deborah Lock based on text from *Tell Me About the World's Religions* (2004) by Lois Rock
This edition copyright © 2021 Lion Hudson IP Limited

Published by
Lion Hudson Limited
Prama House, 267 Banbury Road
Summertown, Oxford OX2 7HT, England
www.lionhudson.com

ISBN 978 0 7459 7968 7
First edition 2021

Acknowledgments
The publisher would like to thank Claire Clinton, Director of Religious Education and RSHE, RE Matters Ltd for consultancy advice.
Scripture quotations are from the Good News Bible © 1994 published by the Bible Societies/HarperCollins Publishers Ltd UK, Good News Bible© American Bible Society 1966, 1971, 1976, 1992. Used with permission.

Picture acknowledgements
Every effort has been made to contact the illustrators of this work, although this has not been possible in all cases. If notified, the publisher will rectify any errors or omissions at the earliest opportunity.

Illustrations
Fred Apps: p. 9; **Lion Hudson Ltd**: pp. 5 (Jacqui Crawford); 1, 43(b) (Javier Joaquin); 11(l) (John Williams); 16 ; 28 (Joy Amsden); **Peter Dennis**: p. 6(r); **Richard Scott**: pp. 6, 12, 13(r), 14, 17(t); **Tony Morris**: p. 15

Photographs
Alamy: pp. 21, 38 (World Religions Photo Library); **Alex Keene/The Walking Camera**: p. 30; **Getty**: p. 4 and front cover (Earl & Nazima Kowall); **Humanists UK**: p. 43(r); **istock**: pp. 6(l) (Mykyta Dolmatov); 10 (nano); 17(l) (Pavliha); 19 (DistinctiveImages); 26 (desifoto); 29 (Jedraszak); 34 (holgs); 37 (life in shots); 39 (Deepak Sethi); 42 (filmstudio); 45 (Idealnabaraj); **Shutterstock**: pp. 8 (Natalia D.); 11(r) (Africa Studio); 20 (ImranShaikh); 22 (Ahmad Faizal Yahya); 23 (Pixeljoy); 25 and back cover, 27 (ninassarts.com); 31 (NeydtStock); 33 (Makmur Asyura); 35 (PhaiApirom); 36(r) (saiko3p); 40 (Hans Wagemaker); 41(l) (Matt Hahnewald); 41(tr) (Arjun bna); 41(br) (Syeda Shad)

A catalogue record for this book is available from the British Library

Printed and bound in China, July 2021, LH54

CONTENTS

What are religions and worldviews? 4

What is Judaism? 6

What do Jews believe? 8

How do Jews live? 10

What is Christianity? 12

What do Christians believe? 14

How do Christians live? 16

What is Islam? 18

What do Muslims believe? 20

How do Muslims live? 22

What is Hinduism? 24

How do Hindus worship? 26

How do Hindus live? 28

What is Buddhism? 30

What do Buddhists believe? 32

How do Buddhists live? 34

What is Sikhism? 36

What do Sikhs believe? 38

How do Sikhs live? 40

What are other worldviews? 42

Glossary 44

Index 46

What are RELIGIONS and WORLDVIEWS?

A worldview is a set of beliefs and practices reflecting a person or group's point of view about the world. A religious worldview is the **belief** in an unseen higher power and is the set of **practices** that believers in that religion follow to express their belief. Religion and worldviews try to answer the important questions people ask, including about life and death and the right thing to do in their everyday lives.

Young girls carry marigolds on plates and wear marigold garlands with traditional dress. This colourful parade is for the Dasai festival in Darjeeling, in India. The festival has Hindu origins, but Buddhists also celebrate it in their own way.

Religious beliefs

Each religion has its own special teachings that become the beliefs of its followers. The teachings can be from the religion's leaders or prophets, which are often written down in holy books. These holy books might also include stories and events in a religion's history. These stories tell people about how their religion has developed and help people understand their situations today.

Religious practices

What people believe affects what they do. People celebrate their beliefs, or religion, by reading holy books, meeting together in special buildings, saying prayers, and performing other rituals. Religion can be important to people at special times, such as at the birth of a baby or the death of someone they love. Religious festivals are celebrated through the year.

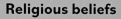

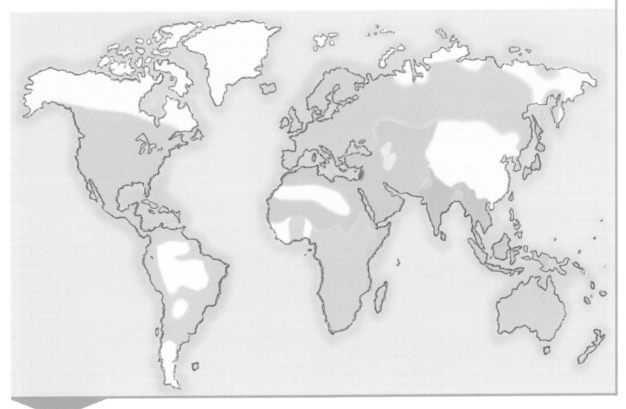

Did you KNOW?

Religions have spread as believers moved to different countries. Nowadays many countries have people from different religions living together.

Q: How many world religions are there?

Religion brings together people who share the same beliefs. There are hundreds of different religions in the world. However, according to world census data, a great many people all over the world belong to the six largest religions. Judaism, Christianity, and Islam are sometimes called Western religions because of where they began. Hinduism, Buddhism, and Sikhism began in countries further east, and are sometimes called Eastern religions. But there are many more religions than these six, for example: Jainism, Bahaism, and Zoroastrianism.

This map shows the places where the six major world religions began and where they first had many followers.

Judaism

Christianity

Islam

Hinduism

Buddhism

Sikhism

Other religions or not many people

What is JUDAISM?

Judaism is one of the oldest world religions, beginning we think nearly 4,000 years ago. The followers are called Jews and they can trace the beginning of their faith to a group of people called **Hebrews**. This people, or family, believed in only one God, unlike those who lived around them. They were later known as the **Israelites**. The story of the Jewish people and what they believe is written in the Hebrew Bible.

The story of Abraham and his descendants can be found in the first book of the Hebrew Bible called Genesis.

The first Hebrews

The Jews believe that a man named Abraham, who was living in the area now known as the Middle East, was chosen by God to become the father of a great people. His son, Isaac, and grandson Jacob, later called Israel, are also known as the patriarchs, or fathers, of Judaism. Jacob had twelve sons, who were to become the fathers of the twelve tribes of Israel.

The Israelites

Many years later, God chose the Israelite, Moses, who became a spokesperson, or prophet, of God's message to the people living in Egypt. Through Moses, God gave the Hebrew people laws to live by. They settled in the land they believed God had given them (modern-day Palestine and Israel). At times, the people did not remember God. When their land was taken, they were forced to live elsewhere, but they returned to their ancient writings and rediscovered living with God. They began meeting together, developing their beliefs and practices, called Judaism.

Q: What is in the Hebrew Bible?

The Hebrew Bible, or Tanakh, is a collection of books that recounts the story of God's relationship with the Jews as his chosen people. The first five books, the Torah, are the most important and contain God's laws. The other books continue the history about Israelite leaders and kings, and God's messages through prophets, known as the Nevi'im. The Ketuvim is a collection of writings that includes poetry and words of wisdom.

Did you KNOW?

The oldest symbol of Judaism is the menorah, a seven-branched gold lampstand, known as the lamp of God. This reminds the Jewish people that they are called to be God's light to all people.

King David was a skilled musician and wrote poems and songs to God, collected in the book of Psalms (Tehillim).

7

What do Jews BELIEVE?

The main belief of all Jews is that there is **one God**. They believe that God made a promise, or covenant, with them. If they kept **God's laws**, God would be their God and they would be God's people, and God would take care of them. The ten most important laws are known as the **Ten Commandments**, given to the prophet Moses.

The Shema is the first prayer that a Jewish child is taught to say.

One God

Talking to God through prayer is important in Jewish life. The most important prayer, the Shema, reminds them of their faith, beginning, *Hear, O Israel, the Lord our God is One.* The words of the Shema are the first to be whispered into the ear of a newborn Jewish baby, and the last that are said to a person who is dying.

God's laws

The Jews count 613 laws in the Torah, the first five books of the Hebrew Bible. These commandments, called mitzvah, are the guide to how to worship God and live in the way that is right and good. These values include being kind and fair to others and taking special care of those in need. The laws cover every aspect of Jewish life, including what can be eaten and how food is prepared, known as kosher. Some Jews follow the laws exactly, while others adapt them for living today.

Q: What are the Ten Commandments?

The Torah states that God gave Moses the ten most important laws on Mount Sinai. **The first four laws are about worshipping God and the others are about treating others in the right way.**

1. I am the Lord your God, who brought you out of Egypt, where you were slaves. Worship no god but me.

2. Do not make for yourselves images of anything in heaven or on earth, or in the water under the earth. Do not bow down to any idol or worship it.

3. Do not use my name for evil purposes.

4. Observe the Sabbath and keep it holy.

5. Respect your father and mother.

6. Do not commit murder.

7. Do not commit adultery.

8. Do not steal.

9. Do not accuse anyone falsely.

10. Do not desire what belongs to another.

Did you KNOW?

The Torah is written on scrolls and is so special that no one can touch it. When people read from the Torah, they follow the words using a special pointer stick called a yad.

Moses carries two stone tablets on which are written the Ten Commandments.

Family life is very important to living the Jewish faith and this is especially shared on the **Sabbath**, a day of rest and focus on God. The **synagogue** is the place where Jews gather to pray and study. Throughout the year, there are **festivals** and special occasions to celebrate.

Did you KNOW?

At the age of thirteen, Jewish boys and girls have a special coming-of-age ceremony in the synagogue called a Bar Mitzvah, for boys, or Bat Mitzvah, for girls. They read aloud in Hebrew from the Torah scrolls.

A Jewish boy reads the Torah on a traditional scroll.

The Sabbath

One of the Jewish laws is about keeping the Shabbat, or Sabbath. This is the one day in the seven days of the week when families relax, remembering that God rested on the seventh day after creating the world. Shabbat begins at sunset on Friday night with the lighting of two candles, a blessing, and then the sharing of an evening meal. On Saturday, some Jews go to the synagogue to meet with others and to worship God. The Shabbat lasts until sunset on Saturday.

Religious practices

The synagogue is the building where Jews gather to pray and meet to study the Hebrew Bible. It is used throughout the week as a meeting place for the Jewish community. On a Saturday, a reading from the Torah is followed by a talk to explain the passage, and psalms of praise to God are sung. The services in the synagogue are led by a rabbi, which means "teacher" in Hebrew.

Q: What are the main Jewish festivals?

Pesach or **Passover** is in spring when the Jews remember how God helped the Israelites, led by Moses, escape from slavery in Egypt. This is an important festival.

Shauvot is held seven weeks after Passover to celebrate when God gave the laws to Moses.

Rosh Hashanah is the Jewish new year at the beginning of October, celebrating new beginnings. Traditionally, a shofar, or ram's horn, is blown. People eat apples and honey to hope for a sweet new year.

Yom Kippur is the Day of Atonement when the Jews ask God to forgive their wrongdoings. This is a very serious day when Jewish people fast from food and drink to show God how sorry they are.

Sukkot is an eight-day harvest festival when some Jews build shelters, remembering the time when the Israelites trusted God to provide for them in the wilderness.

Hanukkah is a festival of lights that celebrates the time when the Temple of Jerusalem was rebuilt, and God's presence was known to be with Jewish people even in difficult times.

Purim in early spring remembers how a queen named Esther saved the Jewish people from being killed.

A shofar or ram's horn is blown at Rosh Hashanah.

The game of dreidel is played during the Jewish holiday of Hanukkah.

What is CHRISTIANITY?

Christianity is the religion of those who believe that a Jew named **Jesus** is the Son of God. The followers of Jesus' teaching are called **Christians** (little Christs), as they believe Jesus is Christ, God's promised king. Their holy book is the **Bible**, which tells of God's plan from the beginning to the end of time.

The life of Jesus

Jesus lived around 2,000 years ago in the time when the Roman empire controlled the land of the Jews (modern-day Palestine and Israel). He grew up in the Jewish faith. When he was about thirty, he journeyed around telling people to become part of "the kingdom of God". The people saw him do miracles, such as healing people with just a touch.

The death of Jesus

Some of the Jewish religious leaders did not like Jesus. They arrested him in Jerusalem and accused him of being a rebel. Jesus was nailed to a wooden cross to die as a criminal by the Romans. He was buried in a tomb but, three days later, Christians believe the body was gone.

The first Christians

Jesus chose twelve disciples, or apostles, from his followers, to whom he explained more things about himself and God. His disciples and others witnessed that, after his death, Jesus appeared alive to them many times before being lifted to heaven. Soon after, they went around spreading the news that Jesus was Christ, the king that God had promised the Jews. They carried on sharing Jesus' teaching about the kingdom of God to people that they met.

Did you KNOW?

The main symbol of Christianity is the cross. A crucifix is the image of Jesus suffering on the cross. An empty cross means hope in the resurrection, for Christians believe Jesus defeated sin (wrongs against God) and death to have everlasting life with God.

Q: What is in the Christian Bible?

The collection of books in the Christian Bible is split into two sections, or testaments. Testaments means "covenant" or "agreement". The Old Testament contains the writings of the Jews from the Hebrew Bible, although some are in a different order. This is about the old agreement God made with people through Moses to keep God's laws. The New Testament begins with four accounts about the life of Jesus, called Gospels, which means "good news". The section continues with a collection of writings by the first Christians. This is the new agreement God made through Jesus.

A man named Paul spread the news about Jesus to many different cities. He wrote letters to keep in touch with these Christians.

What do Christians BELIEVE?

Christians believe in one God, who is Father, Son, and Holy Spirit, known as the **Trinity**. They have a loving relationship with God and believe that they should tell the world about Jesus. They follow his **teachings** and **example** by showing **God's love** and forgiveness to everyone.

Sometimes Jesus taught his followers on the hillsides around Lake Galilee.

Trinity God

The Trinity explains what Christians believe God is like. God is Father, creator and provider of all things. God is Son, who came down from heaven as a human to live among people, known as the incarnation, and to save them from sin and death, known as salvation. God is Holy Spirit, guiding and living in every believer.

God's love

Christians believe that Jesus was sent by God for a special purpose. He was God born into the world to live among all its wrongdoing (sin) that separated people from God. Although Jesus did nothing wrong, he was still put to death by his enemies. Christians believe that when God raised Jesus to life, he showed God's love is stronger than all wrongdoing – strong enough to help people live in the right way and stronger than death. They believe that, through Jesus, people are no longer separated from God.

Q: What did Jesus teach?

Jesus spoke to people about living in the way that was right in God's eyes. He respected the Jewish laws of his faith but focused on two commands:

Love the Lord your God with all your heart, with all your soul, with all your mind, and with all your strength.
Love others as you love yourself.

He told them about God and God's kingdom and how to talk with God through prayer. Jesus taught his followers to say this prayer that sums up his teaching:

Our Father in heaven:
May your holy name be honored;
may your Kingdom come;
may your will be done on earth as it is in heaven.
Give us today the food we need.
Forgive us the wrongs we have done, as we forgive the wrongs that others have done to us.
Do not bring us to hard testing, but keep us safe from the Evil One.

Did you KNOW?

Jesus often taught the crowds using stories that had a special meaning, known as parables.

The parable of the Good Samaritan is about being kind and helpful to everyone.

How do Christians LIVE?

Just like the first followers of Jesus, many Christians often meet in groups, or **churches**, to worship, learn about their faith, and pray together, especially on Sundays. When someone joins the faith, they are **baptized**. They remember Jesus through sharing **bread and wine** together and celebrating **festivals** through the year.

Did you KNOW?

A community of Christians is known as the church, but this also refers to the building where Christians meet. Leaders of church worship have several titles such as priest, vicar, minister, or pastor.

Baptism

When Jesus started his teaching, he was baptized, or dipped, in the River Jordan. New believers and young children are baptized to welcome them into the whole community of the church. The dipping into water is a sign of washing away an old life and starting clean and new as members of life in God's kingdom.

Bread and wine

At the last supper that Jesus had with his friends before he died, Jesus asked them to remember him through the sharing of bread and wine. Many Christians continue to do this to remember that it is because of Jesus that they are part of God's kingdom. This ceremony is called different things in different churches, such as Mass, Eucharist, Holy Communion, and the Lord's Supper.

Shepherds came to see the newborn baby Jesus, lying in a manger.

Q: What are the important Christian festivals?

Christmas remembers Jesus' humble birth in Bethlehem.

Good Friday remembers the day Jesus was crucified in Jerusalem.

This is followed by **Easter** on the Sunday, when Christians celebrate their belief that Jesus rose again. Easter is the most important Christian festival.

Ascension remembers the day Jesus went to heaven: a place with God beyond life.

Pentecost is ten days later and remembers the day when the Holy Spirit gives Jesus' followers the courage to tell others about Jesus.

At a harvest service, Christians give thanks for all the good things God has given them. They often bring food to give to people in need in the community.

17

Followers of Islam are called Muslims and they believe in the One True God. They follow the teachings of a man named **Muhammad**, who was chosen, Muslims believe, to be one of God's **prophets**, or messengers. Their holy book is called the **Qu'ran** and other texts include the Hadith, which tells about Muhammad's life.

A common symbol of Islam is a crescent moon and star.

Prophet Muhammad

In Makkah (Mecca), Saudi Arabia, in 610 CE there was an honest and trusted trader named Muhammad. Muslim people believe that an angel appeared to him and gave the first of many messages from the One God to him. Muhammad shared the messages with his family and friends, but the people of Makkah did not like his preaching, so Muhammad moved to Madinah (Medina) where the religion developed.

The last prophet

Many Muslims believe that Muhammad was the last and greatest in a line of prophets. Earlier prophets included Ibrahim (Abraham) and Musa (Moses) from the Jewish scriptures and Easa (Jesus) from Christian scriptures. Muslims believe that the angel came and took Muhammad on a night journey to Jerusalem to meet the other prophets. After this, he was taken up to be shown heaven.

Q: What is in the Qu'ran?

The Qu'ran, written in Arabic, is the text Muslims believe are the actual words of God that were told to Muhammad over a twenty-three-year period. Muslims respect the words, with many learning them by heart. The Qu'ran is divided into thirty parts and contains 114 chapters, known as suras. Other important texts are the Sunnah and the Hadith that tell of the things Muhammad said and did during his life. The Hadith was written by his companions. These texts guide Muslims in the right way to live.

Muslim children are expected to read the Qu'ran.

The Islamic religion is based on the belief in the **only True God** and the purpose of every person should be to serve God. The word "Islam" in Arabic means "**submission** to the will of God". They believe that Muhammad was the last prophet, and he received the actual **Word of God**.

Only True God

The Arabic word for God is "Allah". There are ninety-nine holy names of God that Muslims use to express the attributes of the One True God. These include the "All-Compassionate", "the Most Merciful", "the Eternal Lord", "the All-Knowing One", and "the All-Seeing One".

Submission

Muslims believe they must do their duty to God, to other people, to their community, and to the Earth itself. For Muslims, only God is perfect, but they aim to live their lives to the best of their abilities. In all things, they must be truthful, honest, respectful, and kind. Many Muslims try to spread the message of Islam to others as they believe only Muslims have a place in paradise: the perfect place to go after death.

If Muslims say the name of the Prophet Muhammad, they follow it with the words, "Peace be upon him", or pbuh, shown here written in Arabic.

Did you KNOW?

The face of Muhammad is never shown, as Islam forbids the making of statues or pictures of the human face because they might be treated in the wrong way and worshipped.

Q: How is the Word of God written?

The words of the Qu'ran in Arabic script are often beautifully written on tiles to cover the walls of some mosques and on other objects. The writing of the text is done with care and respect, as Muslims believe they are the actual Word of God given to Prophet Muhammad. The opening chapter of the Qu'ran is the Sura Al-fatihah:

All praise belongs to Allah, Lord of all the worlds,
the All-beneficent, the All-merciful, Master of the Day
of Judgement.
You alone do we worship and to You alone do we turn
for help.
Guide us on the straight path, the path of those whom
You have blessed
– such as have not incurred Your wrath, nor are astray.

An illustrated Qu'ran.

Muslims show their love and obedience to God by doing five things, which are known as the **Five Pillars of Islam**. The Muslim community meet and pray together in a **mosque** or masjid, especially on Fridays. Through the year, two important **festivals of Eid** celebrate significant events.

The Ka'bah is a stone building dedicated to God and covered in a black cloth decorated with verses from the Qu'ran.

The Five Pillars of Islam

There are five "pillars" required of every Muslim through their lives.

The **Shahada** are the Arabic words Muslims say to declare their faith. In English these words are, "There is no god but Allah; Muhammad is the messenger of Allah." These words are whispered in a baby's ear at birth and are the last words said at the time of death.

The **Salah** are the five set times of prayer during the day. Before prayer, Muslims must wash in a certain way. Wherever they are in the world, Muslims face Makkah to pray and follow a certain order of words and movements.

The **Sawm** is a time of not eating or drinking (fasting) from dawn to dusk. This happens during the Islamic month of Ramadan. Muslims are showing their obedience to God by doing this.

The **Zakah** is a payment made to the poor, people in need, and important works. A Muslim believes that all their riches belong to God, so a part of their wealth is given to what is important to God.

The **Hajj** is a pilgrimage to Makkah that takes place every year. Every Muslim must do the Hajj at least once in their life. Muslims from around the world visit the Ka'bah in Makkah to praise God together and renew their faith.

Festivals of Eid

The **Eid-ul-Adha** is celebrated on the last day of the Hajj and remembers the time when Ibrahim (Abraham) had a dream to sacrifice his son as an act of obedience to Allah (God). Allah stopped him and gave a lamb to sacrifice instead. The **Eid-ul-Fitr** is the celebration to mark the end of Ramadan, the time of fasting. Muslims say prayers of thanks, give to the poor, and give gifts to friends and family.

Q: What happens at a mosque?

The main part of a mosque is the prayer hall. This is open all through the week, but every Friday at noon Muslim men are required to attend prayers. They face a niche in the wall, known as the mihrab, that marks the direction of Makkah. The prayers are led by an imam, who also gives a talk. The mosque also provides a place to study and discuss the Qu'ran, and is where charity work is organized.

Did you KNOW?

The highest point of many mosques is the minaret, from which is heard the call to prayer. The call to prayer, or adhan, is announced by a man known as the muezzin.

This is the Sharif Hussein Bin Ali mosque in Aqaba, Jordan.

What is HINDUISM?

Hinduism began near the River Indus in India more than 4,000 years ago, but its **beliefs** go back many thousands of years earlier. The worshippers are called Hindus and they believe that God, known as **Brahman**, is everywhere and is truth. There are two main types of **holy books**: the Shruti and the Smriti.

Did you KNOW?

The symbol of Hinduism is the Aum, or Om, which is a very special sound in Hinduism. Out of this sound, Hindus believe the universe began and to say the sound is to agree that Brahman is all in all.

The sacred symbol Aum is used at the beginning and end of Hindu books, and can be found on many everyday objects in Hindu homes.

Hindu beliefs

Hindus believe that the soul, the atman, is on a journey. They believe in rebirth, or reincarnation, which means the soul leaves one body at death and is reborn as an animal or as a person. The next life depends on how they lived in their last life. This journey can last through many lifetimes to reach the final goal of being one with Brahman, known as heaven.

Brahman

The one God of Hindus is called Brahman. Brahman is beyond everything, but Brahman is within everything, and within each human soul. The many gods and goddesses of Hinduism are all just parts of the one Brahman. The three most important ways of understanding Brahman are the gods: Brahma, the creator; Vishnu, the protector; and Shiva, the destroyer.

Q: What is in Hindus' holy books?

One type of holy book is the Shruti, which means "that which is heard". These books are believed to come from the gods and are called Vedas and Upanishads. The Vedas are hymns written in Sanskrit writing. The Upanishads are conversations between a teacher, or guru, and his disciple. The other type of holy book is the Smriti, which means "that which is remembered". These books include tales by storytellers, such as the Ramayana and the Mahabharata. These stories feature Vishnu, who takes a human form known as an avatar. In this incarnation, Vishnu comes to Earth to help put things right and give guidance.

Vishnu's avatars include Rama, who defeats a demon king, and Krishna the farmer, who becomes a great soldier and ruler.

How do Hindus WORSHIP?

An important part of Hinduism is worship, called puja. Some worship is done in the **temple**, or mandir, where ceremonies are led by a priest. Most Hindu worship is done at home around a **shrine**. Every temple and shrine has a statue or picture, known as a murti, of one of the **Hindu gods and goddesses**.

Most Hindus have shrines in their homes with a picture or statue of their chosen deity.

Temple worship

The priest begins the worship by "waking" the temple god with a ceremonial bath and then dresses the statue in clothes and jewels and makes offerings. Then the curtains that separate the room from the main part of the temple are drawn back and other ceremonies take place. These ceremonies include singing hymns, dancing to the music of bells and tambourines, readings, and prayers for the community. Hindus bring gifts of flowers or food to offer the god, which are then later given to those visiting the temple and the poor.

A shrine at home

In every Hindu home, there is a prayer room or a small place set aside as a shrine. The worshipper washes and puts on clean clothes and then they pray that the god, who is already in the person's heart, will come into the house and stay for the worship. The image of the god is washed and decorated, a lamp is lit, and incense burned. Food is offered and prayers are said for family and friends.

Q: What are some popular Hindu gods and goddesses?

Vishnu protects the universe and Lakshmi is the goddess of wealth and good fortune. Their incarnations, or avatars, as people on Earth include Lord Rama and his wife Sita.

Shiva is destroyer and re-creator, and is often shown as "Lord of the Dance", who controls the cycle of life. His companion goddesses are violent Kali, gentle Parvati, and powerful Durga.

Hanuman, the monkey god, is a symbol of all that is strong and energetic.

Ganesha, the elephant god, is a symbol of all that is strong and wise.

Did you KNOW?

Hindu worship uses all five senses: a bell to wake the god, food offerings, an image or statue of the god, burning incense to purify the air, and kum-kum powder as a mark of respect on the forehead. The powder is red, which represents purity in Asia.

Ganesha, the elephant god.

How do Hindus LIVE?

For Hindus, all of life is part of the journey of the soul to become one with Brahman. There are many ways of reaching this final goal, known as **moksha**. There are **sixteen samskars**, or ceremonies, marking stages in a person's life. Throughout the year, there are many **festivals** linked to the Hindu's popular gods.

Ways to moksha

Hindus try to break out of the cycle of life, death, and rebirth by their actions. One way is to faithfully worship, another is to control the mind and the body by yoga. One of the hardest ways is to understand all the holy books with the help of a teacher, or guru. The way of karma means actions affect the next life, so good and kind deeds bring a person closer to the end of the journey.

Sixteen samskars

Many Hindus believe the stages of a person's life help them to find happiness and ceremonies mark these moments. The first three are before birth. The fourth happens when a baby is born and the aum is marked on the tongue with a golden pen dipped in honey. Other ceremonies happen through childhood and some are linked with marriage. The last is the funeral, when the body is cremated by burning to ashes.

Hindus believe that several rivers in India are holy, especially the River Ganges. Many will make the journey, or pilgrimage, to wash in them to receive a special blessing.

Q: What are stories celebrated at Hindu festivals?

Diwali is the festival of lights that happens in October or November. Hindus light candles to invite Lakshmi, the goddess of wealth, to visit their homes and bring good luck. Hindus remember the triumph of Vishnu's avatar, Rama, over the ten-headed demon king Ravana, who had taken Rama's wife, Sita.

Holi is the festival to celebrate spring and new life. Hindus remember Vishnu's avatar, Krishna, visiting Earth to triumph over evil Holika. Hindus throw powder paint and coloured water.

Mahashivrati celebrates Shiva rising from the underworld. Hindus fast and pray through the night, remembering when Shiva performed the cosmic dance from creation to destruction.

Janmashtami celebrates the birth of Lord Krishna, Vishnu's avatar, and the story of his escape and rescue from an evil king. A trail of tiny footprints may be drawn.

Did you KNOW?

In Hinduism, cows are treated as holy and allowed to roam freely in the streets. At certain festivals, they are often decorated with garlands of flowers and bells.

It is partly because Vishnu's avatar, Krishna, at first looked after cows that every cow is treated as holy among Hindus.

Buddhism began around 2,500 years ago with the teachings of a prince called **Siddhartha Gautama**. He became known as the **Buddha** and his followers are called Buddhists. Buddhists try to achieve **enlightenment** through the way they live, and perfect peace. Their holy book is called the Tipitaka and includes the **Pali Canon**.

Most Buddhist temples contain impressive statues of the Buddha.

Prince Siddhartha

In a tiny kingdom in southern Nepal, Prince Siddhartha Guatama grew up never leaving the grounds of his palace. At sixteen he married and for thirteen years lived happily. But he was curious about his kingdom. When he went beyond the palace walls, he first saw an old man, then a sick person, and then a funeral procession. He sadly realized he would not be young, strong, and live forever. Then he saw a serene and happy holy man, a beggar monk, and set out to learn wisdom.

Buddha, the enlightened one

While Siddhartha rested under the shade of a bodhi, or fig tree, he believed he finally understood the answer to the problem of suffering in the world. He became "fully awake" to reality and became the Buddha, the enlightened one. He began to teach others and they became the first disciples, beginning a community of monks, known as the Sangha.

Did you KNOW?

Statues of Buddha often show him in a crossed-legged position, the lotus position. The hands may be shown in his lap in a meditation (relaxed) position. A raised hand means fearlessness and blessing.

Q: What is in the Pali Canon?

The teachings of the Buddha were handed down by word of mouth long before they were written down. The writings are known as the Tipitaka, which means "three baskets", as they were made on palm leaves and stored in baskets. One collection was written in Pali, the language of Buddha, and is called the Pali Canon. This contains the teachings of the Buddha and his companions, comments, and rules for monks.

The bodhi or fig tree is also known as the Tree of Wisdom.

What do Buddhists BELIEVE?

Buddhists believe that nothing in the world lasts forever and wishing things did causes the world's suffering. Buddha's teachings, or dharma, to explain this are called the **Four Noble Truths**. Followers of Buddha seek to follow his **Eightfold Path to enlightenment**, beyond suffering to find perfect peace, known as **nirvana**.

Did you KNOW?

The symbol of Buddhism is a wheel of life as the cycle of life, death, and rebirth. The wheel has eight spokes, reminding followers of the Eightfold Path to enlightenment. This is known as the wheel of Dharma.

The Eightfold Path

The first two steps require wisdom:
1. Right understanding with the Four Noble Truths.
2. Right thoughts with a commitment to live with love towards others.

The next three steps require morality:
3. Right speech that is pure and kind, avoiding gossip, lying, and angry words.
4. Right action by doing good and showing loving kindness.
5. Right livelihood by choosing work that is peace-making and does no harm to living things.

The last three steps are linked to training the mind, or meditation:
6. Right effort by getting rid of bad thoughts and replacing them with good ones.
7. Right mindfulness through being aware of oneself and of the needs of others.
8. Right concentration by learning to meditate to become calm and peaceful.

Four Noble Truths

1. At the heart of everything is suffering, or dukkha.
2. Suffering exists because people are always wanting things and never happy with what they have.
3. Suffering ends when people let go of the wanting.
4. To get rid of suffering, people must follow the Eightfold Path.

Q: What is nirvana?

Buddhists believe that there is a cycle of birth, life, death, and rebirth. This continues until someone gains enlightenment. When all want and suffering is gone, the cycle is broken, as the person has reached nirvana. It is the place of perfect peace, happiness, and freedom from suffering.

A raindrop inspired this Tibetan Buddhist proverb:

This life is as the tiny splash of a raindrop: a thing of beauty that disappears as soon as it comes into being. So set your goal clearly and make right use of every day and every night.

33

Buddhists follow Buddha's **five rules** of how to live well so that they can avoid suffering and bad feelings. They go to temples, known as pagodas or stupas, and make shrines in their homes, to **meditate and study** the life and teachings of Buddha. Many Buddhists join **monasteries** to live a simple spiritual life.

Buddhists celebrate the Floating Candle Festival in November. Candles are put in tiny cups made from leaves or paper and floated on a river to symbolize letting go of hate and anger.

Five Rules

All Buddhists try to follow the Five Rules of good actions:

1. Do not harm or kill any living thing.
2. Do not take anything that belongs to others.
3. Do not indulge the body.
4. Do not lie or gossip.
5. Do not drink alcohol or take drugs, which cloud the mind.

Meditation and study

The Buddha was not a god and taught there was no god. Even so, many Buddhists have statues of Buddha and bow before it as a sign of respect. They also meditate to focus the mind, and study and listen to Buddhist teachings. There are special festivals each month at the full moon when Buddhists go to the temples. Between **Dharma Day**, when Buddha gave his first sermon, and **Sangha Day**, Buddhists make an extra effort to deepen their understanding of Buddha's teachings.

Did you KNOW?

Wesak is the festival celebrating the birth, the enlightenment, and the death of the Buddha. Buddhists decorate their houses and temples with many candles.

Buddhist monks meditating.

Q: What is the life of a Buddhist monk or nun?

Buddhists give thanks for three key things that help them in their faith, known as the Three Jewels: the Buddha, the Dharma (teaching) and the Sangha, which is the Buddhist community of monks and nuns. These monks and nuns own nothing and rely on other Buddhists to give them food, clothing, and other necessities. They can only eat two meals a day. They follow many rules and spend their time studying the Dharma and meditating. They give spiritual help to other Buddhists. Some stay for a short time, while others stay for life.

What is SIKHISM?

Sikhism, or Sikhi, began about 500 years ago when a man named **Nanak** believed he was being called by God to be a religious leader, known as a **guru**. The followers of Sikhism are called Sikhs and they believe in one God, known as Sat Guru, who is in everyone and is everywhere. Their holy book is the **Guru Granth Sahib**.

Did you KNOW?

The symbol of Sikhism is called the Khanda. It is made up of a straight-edged sword, a ring, and two curved swords. These represent God's power, justice, truth, and infinity.

The Khanda Monument in New Delhi is a symbol of the Sikh faith.

Guru Nanak

Nanak was born in 1469 near Lahore, Pakistan. His family were Hindus. People said he was a thoughtful and wise child and he liked talking to the wandering holy men from the Hindu and Islamic faiths. At the age of thirty, he was bathing in the River Bein when he felt himself being carried up to heaven. Three days later he returned to his family and said that God had called him to be a guru, a teacher, showing people how to find God for themselves. He set up the community of the Sikhs.

The ten gurus

Before he died, Nanak chose a man, known as Guru Angad, to be the next leader of the community. Each leader or guru chose the next to follow him. Each guru continued to develop the Sikh faith. The tenth guru, Guru Gobind Singh, was the last person to be called a guru in Sikhism. He declared the holy book was to be the guru ever after.

Gurpurbs are festivals that remember their lives.

Q: What is in the Guru Granth Sahib?

The Guru Granth Sahib is the holy book of the Sikhs. The book contains sacred hymns, known as Shabads, about wisdom and teachings from the Sikh gurus, as well as a few Hindu and Muslim poets. The Guru Granth Sahib is respected as a living guru. The Sikhs treat the book as a highly respected teacher, which includes bowing before it, covering their heads, removing shoes, and providing cushions and a canopy for the Guru Granth. This reflects how they would treat a king or leader 500 years ago.

The chauri is a fan made from yak tail hair that is waved over the Guru Granth Sahib when it is read or carried in a procession.

What do Sikhs BELIEVE?

Sikhs believe in one God as declared in the first statement of the Guru Granth Sahib called the **Mool Mantar**. They believe God is beyond everything but within each person, so it is important to think about, or **meditate**, about God. Sikhs believe that God will guide them to lead a good life.

The Mool Mantar is twelve words in the Punjabi language, written in Gurmukhi.

The Mool Mantar

This is the first hymn in the Sikh's holy book, which is about God: *There is only one God. Truth is his name. He is the creator. He is without fear. He is without hate. He is timeless and without form. He is beyond death, the enlightened one. He can be known by the Guru's grace.*

Meditation

By saying the Nam, the name of God, and meditating on it, Sikhs believe each person can know God more and more. Through meditation, Sikhs learn to live this life as God wants: living honestly and working hard, treating everyone as equal, loving and serving one another, and being generous to those in need. Sikhs meditate at any possible moment during the day.

Q: How does a Sikh meditate?

Sikhs believe they must think, or meditate, on God's name so that they become fully one with God, or enlightened. Sometimes they sing hymns or listen to readings from the holy book, the Guru Granth Sahib. Or they just sit quietly on their own, repeating God's name over and over. In this way each person can break out of the cycle of reincarnation – being born again and again in different forms – and find enlightenment, called nirvana.

Did you KNOW?

The word "Sikh" comes from a word meaning "disciple".

A Sikh man sits in a relaxed position to meditate.

How do Sikhs LIVE?

Living as a community, or **Khalsa**, is very important for Sikhs. There are five things that show a person is a member, called the **five Ks**. Sikhs worship in a temple called the **gurdwara** (house of the guru) and, after a service, everyone shares a meal in the kitchen, or **langar**.

The gurdwara known as the Golden Temple was built by the fifth Guru in the middle of a lake in northern India.

The Khalsa

The tenth guru set up a community of Sikhs, or Khalsa, meaning "Community of the Pure". They were a group of men who were willing to fight to defend their faith. Today the community includes men and women as equals. At the joining ceremony, called baptism, each new member drinks a special sugar water, called amrit, and after this wears the five Ks.

Gurdwara worship

Sikhs meet in a simple building called the gurdwara, or "gateway to the guru", to worship. The holy book, the Guru Granth Sahib, is kept raised up on cushions under a canopy. People sit on the floor and listen to readings, and chant prayers and hymns. Afterwards they share a meal in the kitchen, or langar, and everyone is welcome to eat the food. Sikhs believe serving others is a way of serving God, known as seva.

Q: What are the five Ks?

Every member of the Sikh community follows the five Ks to show they belong:

Kesh – members do not cut their hair or shave their beard to show they accept God's way.

Kirpan – members have a symbolic sword to show they are willing to defend their faith.

Kangha – members have a comb to show the importance of cleanliness.

Kara – members wear a steel bracelet as a reminder that the link between God and them is unbreakable.

Kachera – members wear traditional shorts as underwear as a reminder of self-control.

Did you KNOW?

Every male member of the Khalsa takes the name Singh, which means "lion". Every female is called Kaur, which means "princess".

The Kesh, Kirpan, and Kara are three of the five Ks.

What are other WORLDVIEWS?

Through history, and still today, there are people who have **no religious faith** but hold views and values that shape their lives. They also often show great kindness and compassion, risking their lives to bring peace and justice to the world. There are many values shared by religious and non-religious people, including **respect and tolerance** for one another.

The Scouting movement is made up of members of different faiths and no faiths, and based on a set of values, including respect and friendship.

Non-religious worldviews

People who are agnostic believe that the existence of God cannot be proved. People who are atheists do not believe in God or gods. A type of atheistic worldview is Humanism, which is a set of values of how people should live or act without following a religion.

Respect and tolerance

Religious people often say that their faith is like a light, showing them the way to live and helping them make decisions. People who have no religious faith find inspiration and guidance from the people and the world around them. Communities have many different organizations and clubs, such as schools and sports teams, that are non-religious but are places where those with or without faith meet. People find shared values to get along with each other.

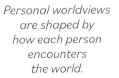

Did you KNOW?

The symbol of Humanism is called the "Happy Human", reflecting the belief that humans should look after each other and themselves.

Q: What are Humanism values?

Think for yourself, act for everyone. Humanists believe that people have one life to live to its fullness. They focus on being happy and a sense of community. It is their duty to support friends and those in need to help them to be happy too. They value thinking and studying science to explain the world around them. Being good friends, being honest, and sharing are some of the values for making a better place for everyone. They celebrate special times for family and friends, such as birthdays. Their ceremonies, such as marriages and funerals, are unique as they are designed and written by those taking part.

Personal worldviews are shaped by how each person encounters the world.

43

GLOSSARY

Atonement: a making up after doing wrong.

Avatar: the appearance of a god in a human body.

Ceremony: a celebration of an occasion, often with set words and actions.

Community: a group of people living in the same place or area, or share a view.

Disciple: a person who follows the way of life and teachings of a religious leader.

Faith: trust in a set of beliefs of a religion, rather than proof.

Fasting: going without food and drink.

Festival: a day or days of celebration, often for religious reasons.

Funeral: a ceremony held for people who have died.

Incarnation: God or gods taking on a human form.

Meditation: focus of the mind.

Obedience: follow a request or law given by another in authority as a duty and with respect.

Parable: a simple story with a deeper spiritual meaning.

Pilgrimage: a journey, often walking, to a holy place as an act of prayer or devotion to God or gods.

Prayer: words said to praise, give thanks, talk, and listen to God or gods.

Prophet: a person who speaks in the name of God.

Religion: the belief in an unseen higher power and the set of practices followed for worship.

Reincarnation: rebirth by the soul being born again in a different body in a cycle of life and death.

Resurrection: raised from the death and come back to life.

Ritual: a religious practice with a series of actions in a certain order.

Scriptures: holy writings thought to be inspired by or the actual words of God or religious leader.

Worship: an act of showing adoration and praise to God or gods.

A father blesses his daughter during the Dashain festival, celebrated by Hindus in Nepal.

Abraham 7, 18, 23

agnostic 42

Allah 20–23

amrit 40

angel 18

Arabic 19–22

Ascension 17

atheist 42

Aum (Om) 24, 28

baptism 16, 40

Bar Mitzvah 8, 10

Bat Mitzvah 8, 10

Brahma 24

Brahman 24, 28

bread and wine 16

Buddha 30–32, 34–35

Buddhism 5, 30–35

Buddhists 4, 30–35

chauri 37

Christian Bible 12, 13

Christianity 5, 12–17

Christians 12–17

Christmas 17

church 16

community 10, 16, 17, 20, 22, 26, 30, 35, 36, 40, 41, 43, 44

covenant 8, 13

cows 15

cross 12, 13

crucifixion 12, 13, 17

Dharma 32, 35

Dharma Day 34

Diwali

Easter 17

Eid-ul-Adha 23

Eid-ul-Fitr 23

Eightfold Path 32, 33

enlightenment 30, 32, 33, 35, 39

Eucharist 16

fast 11, 22, 23, 29, 44

Five Ks 40–41

Five Pillars of Islam 22

Five Rules 34

Floating Candle 34

Four Noble Truths 32–33

Friday 10, 22, 23

Ganesha 27

God's kingdom 12, 15, 16

God's laws 6, 7, 8–9, 13

Good Friday 17

Gospels 13

gurdwara 40

Gurpurbs 36

guru 25, 28, 36–37, 40

Guru Granth Sahib 36, 37, 38, 39, 40

Hadith 18, 19

Hajj 22, 23

Hanukkah 11

Hanuman 27

Happy Human 43

harvest 11, 17

heaven 9, 12, 14, 15, 17, 18, 24, 36

Hebrew Bible 6, 7, 8, 10

Hijrah 19

Hinduism 4, 5, 24–29

Hindus 24–29

Holi 29

Holy Communion 16

Holy Spirit 14, 17

Humanism 42, 43

imam 23

incarnation 14, 25, 27, 44

Islam 5, 18–23

Janmashtami 29

Jerusalem 11, 12, 17, 18

Jesus 12–17, 18

Jews 6–11, 12–13

Judaism 5, 6–11

Ka'bah 22

Kachera 41

Kangha 41

Kara 41

karma 28

Kaur 41

Kesh 41

Ketuvim 7

Khalsa 40

Khanda 36

Kirpan 41

Krishna 25, 29

Lakshmi 27, 29

Lord's Prayer 15

Lord's Supper 16

Madinah (Medina) 18, 19

Mahabharata 25

Mahashivrati 29

Makkah (Mecca) 18, 19, 22, 23

marriage 28, 43

Mass 16

meditation 32, 34, 38, 44

menorah 7

minister 16

moksha 28

Mool Mantar 38

monastery 34

monks 30, 31, 35

Moses 6, 8, 9, 11, 13, 18

mosque (masjid) 21, 22, 23

Muhammad 18–21, 22

murti 26

Muslims 18–23

Nam 38

Nanak 36

Nevi'im 7

nirvana 32, 33, 39

Pali Canon 30, 31

parables 15, 44

paradise 20

Pentecost 17

Pesach 11

pilgrimage 22, 28, 44

prayer 4, 8, 15, 22, 23, 26, 40, 44

priest 16, 26

prophet 4, 6, 7, 8, 18, 20, 21, 44

proverb 33

puja 26

Purim 11

Qu'ran 18, 19, 21, 22, 23

rabbi 10

Rama 25, 27, 29

Ramadan 22, 23

Ramayana 25

reincarnation 24, 39, 44

resurrection 13

River Bein 36

River Ganges 28

Rosh Hashanah 11

Sabbath 9, 10

Salah 22

samskars 28

Sangha 30, 35

Sangha Day 34

Sanskrit 25

Sat Guru 36

Saturday 10

Sawm 22

seva 40

Shabads 37

Shabbat 10

Shahada 22

Shauvot 11

Shema 8

Shiva 24, 27, 29

shrine 26, 34

Shruti 24, 25

Siddhartha Gautama 30

Sikhism (Sikhi) 5, 36–41

Sikhs 36–41

singh 41

Sita 27, 29

Smriti 24, 25

Sukkot 11

Sunday 16, 17

Sunnah 19

Sura Al-fatihah 21

synagogue 10

Tanakh 7

temple 11, 26, 30, 34, 35, 40

Ten Commandments 8, 9

Tipitaka 30, 31

Torah 7, 8, 9, 10

Trinity 14

Upanishads 25

Vedas 25

Vishnu 24, 25, 27, 29

Wesak 35

wheel of Dharma 32

worship 8, 9, 10, 16, 26–27, 28, 40, 44

yoga 28

Yom Kippur 11

Zakah 22

Other titles in the KEYWORDS series:

What's in the Bible?

ISBN 978 0 7459 7966 3

What Did Jesus Do?

ISBN 978 0 7459 7967 0